Original title:

The Art of Heartfelt Apologies

Author: Mirell Mesipuu

ISBN HARDBACK: 978-9916-89-211-4

ISBN PAPERBACK: 978-9916-89-212-1

ISBN EBOOK: 978-9916-89-213-8

Painting Over Past Mistakes

With every stroke, I begin anew,
Colors blend where pain once grew.
A canvas stretched beneath my hand,
I reshape fears, I take a stand.

The brush whispers secrets of lost time,
Melodies of hope start to chime.
Shadows fade with each bright hue,
Regret dissolves; I find what's true.

Each layer hides a tale of old,
In vibrant tones, I break the mold.
Mistakes now soften with each pass,
Transformed in beauty, none could surpass.

I paint the sun where darkness lay,
A vivid dawn breaks through the gray.
With every color, lessons learn,
In my heart, a new fire burns.

So here I stand, a master now,
No fear of flaws, just take a bow.
My past a canvas, bold and wide,
I paint my dreams, and let them ride.

The Grace in Owning Mistakes

In the quiet moments, we stand still,
Reflecting on the choices that highlight will.
Mistakes are threads in our life's design,
We learn to weave them, making us fine.

Facing our faults, we grow anew,
Each stumble a step, a path we pursue.
In vulnerability, we find our strength,
The grace in owning, we lengthen our length.

Navigating the Depths of Understanding

In the sea of thoughts, we set our sail,
Diving deep where emotions prevail.
Waves of confusion, we try to parse,
Seeking clarity, our thoughts, we disburse.

Conversations flow like a gentle tide,
In every question, let honesty guide.
With each heartbeat, connection grows,
Navigating depths where true wisdom flows.

The Rebirth of Trust

From ashes of doubt, new bonds ignite,
Like dawn breaking through the endless night.
With whispers of hope, we build again,
The warmth of commitment, where love has lain.

With fragile hearts, we step back in,
Rekindling the fire, letting light in.
Through patience and kindness, we mend the rift,
In the rebirth of trust, our spirits lift.

A Symphony of Empathy

In the orchestra of voices, we take part,
Each note a feeling, a shared heart.
Listening closely, we tune our ears,
Together we rise, connecting through tears.

The melody of kindness, soft and clear,
In every echo, we draw near.
Harmony blossoms as we understand,
A symphony of empathy, hand in hand.

Bridges Built with Tears

Across the river, dreams do flow,
Made of sorrow, hurt, and woe.
In every drop, a story shared,
Fragile memories that once dared.

Yet with each tear, a bridge is formed,
Uniting hearts, though battered and worn.
They span the gap from grief to hope,
Where we find strength, learn to cope.

Notes from a Distant Heart

In the silence, whispers call,
Echoes of love, they rise and fall.
Each note a promise, gently spun,
Hopes held close, but never won.

Fingers trace the lines of fate,
Time apart, it cannot wait.
Through woven words, we seek the light,
Guiding us through the darkest night.

Chasing Shadows of Mistakes

In twilight's glow, regret takes flight,
Chasing shadows into the night.
Each misstep carved in fragile stone,
Lessons learned when we're alone.

Yet shadows fade with morning's grace,
What once was lost, we can embrace.
With every dawn, a chance to mend,
To rise above, and start again.

Threads of Oath and Honesty

Woven tightly, threads of trust,
In honesty, we find what's just.
Each promise made, a binding tie,
Strength in words, we can't deny.

Through trials faced, we stand as one,
Together stronger, battles won.
With every thread, a story spun,
In unity, our hearts are one.

Patchwork of a Pained Soul

In shadows cast by memories,
Fragments of a restless past.
Stitched together with silence,
But the pain, it holds steadfast.

A heart that wears its scars well,
Each stitch tells a story bold.
Colors fade with every tear,
Yet the quilt still feels the cold.

Echoes of laughter linger,
Haunted by what could have been.
A tapestry of longing,
Woven through the skin.

A patchwork made of sorrow,
Yet bright threads weave the light.
In the silence of the night,
Hope flickers, soft and slight.

Though the seams may fray and break,
And the colors start to blur,
In the chaos lies a beauty,
That only pain can stir.

The Weight of Unsaid Words

Bottled feelings, tight inside,
Heavy is the heart's refrain.
Thoughts collide, yet lips stay sealed,
Bearing witness to the pain.

Eyes convey what words cannot,
A glance that lingers, waits.
In moments filled with quiet dread,
Time conspires, while fate bates.

Each hesitation echoes loud,
A silence sharp as glass.
Between the breaths, a message forms,
Yet courage seems to pass.

In corridors of silence,
Dreams decay beneath the strain.
What if words were never spoken?
Could they still be felt in vain?

Heavy lies the heart's burden,
Unvoiced truths, a tangled thread.
In the end, will we regret,
All the things we left unsaid?

A Dance of Lost Trust

In a room where shadows linger,
Trust once sparkled like the sun.
Steps once taken now feel burdened,
With each turn, the trust is gone.

Whispers wrapped in gentle lies,
Promises made under the stars.
Yet the music fades to silence,
As the hearts draw invisible bars.

Hands that used to clasp in faith,
Now tremble in the quiet hum.
Footsteps echo, distant, cold,
Where the dance of love succumbed.

Hope once danced on fragile dreams,
Now lies crumpled on the floor.
With each waltz, we lose the beat,
A rhythm we can't restore.

In the end, we learn to let go,
Of the love that's turned to dust.
With heavy hearts, we part in silence,
In this dance of lost, lost trust.

Silent Soliloquy

In the corners of my mind,
Thoughts drift like autumn leaves.
Whispers echo in the dark,
A soliloquy that grieves.

Each emotion, tightly wound,
Yet, expression finds no home.
In silence, the truth unfolds,
But in shadows, I still roam.

Words that taste like bitter rain,
Fall softly on the restless ground.
In the stillness, there's a plea,
For a voice to break the sound.

Hidden dreams and weary hopes,
Float upon the breath of night.
Silent soliloquy within,
Yearns for dawn's redeeming light.

But until the sun breaks free,
And the silence starts to fade,
I'll wander through my thoughts alone,
In this quiet serenade.

Reconstructing the Shattered

In fragments scattered wide,
Hope glimmers in the haze.
We gather each lost shard,
Building brighter days.

With tender hands we strive,
To piece the puzzle true.
Each cut a memory,
A lesson learned anew.

The tears like raindrops fall,
Yet strength grows through the pain.
We forge our hearts in fire,
And rise to love again.

From ruins we create,
A vision of our dreams.
A tapestry of life,
Unraveled at the seams.

With every breath we take,
We breathe in all we've lost.
To build anew, we learn,
And cherish every cost.

Tattered Pieces

Among the scattered dreams,
Lie tattered pieces small.
Each fragment holds a tale,
Of rise, of stumble, fall.

We hold them in our hands,
Like treasures of the past.
Repairing every tear,
Ensuring love will last.

With stitches made of hope,
And threads spun from our fears,
We craft a brighter path,
Through laughter and through tears.

Each piece once torn apart,
Now dances in the air.
Reclaimed through time and grace,
Together we must share.

In artless harmony,
A symphony of hearts.
The tattered pieces blend,
Creating brighter parts.

Mending Whole

With every stitch we take,
We mend the broken seams.
In patience, love unfolds,
Restoring all our dreams.

The cracks may tell a tale,
Of battles fought with grace.
Yet in the midst of strife,
We find a warm embrace.

Through fleeting moments, we,
Repair what once was lost.
Unearthing hidden scars,
To cherish what it costs.

Our hearts a patchwork quilt,
Of stories intertwined.
Each square a memory,
Of love that we can find.

In unity we stand,
Reformed and whole again.
Together in the light,
Our souls shall ever reign.

Beneath the Veil of Apologies

Beneath the heavy veil,
Of whispers, hearts await.
A longing for the truth,
To cleanse the lingering weight.

Each word a fragile hope,
The air thick with regret.
Yet courage lights the path,
For moments we forget.

With every bowed heads low,
We seek redemption's grace.
To lift the weight of sorrow,
And find a safe embrace.

The veil begins to lift,
Revealing tender hearts.
Unraveling the pain,
As healing slowly starts.

In vulnerability,
We find our strength anew.
Beneath the veil of scars,
We learn just what is true.

The Currency of Regret

In shadows of the past,
Regrets like coins we hold.
Each one a haunting echo,
Of stories left untold.

We barter with our tears,
And trade our silent sighs.
For moments lost in time,
Underneath indifferent skies.

Yet through this heavy weight,
We learn to value grace.
The currency of love,
Can fill the empty space.

In reflections we find peace,
As lessons intertwine.
Each loss, a hidden gain,
Transformed in bittersweet rhyme.

So let us cast aside,
The weight of what's been spent.
Embrace the now with hope,
And mend what time has bent.

Inking Kindness into Apologies

A pen in hand, a heart laid bare,
Words flow softly, light as air.
Each stroke a bridge, a tender start,
In every letter, I mend my heart.

Mistakes are shadows, fading fast,
With every ink, we can outlast.
Forgiveness blooms, it's pure and bright,
In the garden of wrongs, we find the light.

Let kindness weave through every line,
In the tapestry of time, we shine.
An artful grace, a humble plea,
In ink, our truths set free.

Beneath the surface, love can grow,
With simple words, we learn to show.
A promise written, a vow renewed,
In ink, our spirits are imbued.

So here's to apologies, sincere and true,
Crafted softly, just for you.
May every page hold love's embrace,
Inking kindness, we find our place.

The Pathway to Amends

Step by step, we walk the way,
Each footfall marks what we say.
On this path, the past is shed,
In every word, the heart is fed.

Hurdles rise, but we won't sway,
With hands held tight, we'll find our way.
A journey shared, a hopeful sigh,
Towards the dawn, we learn to fly.

Side by side, the world feels light,
Healing whispers, day turns bright.
In this moment, let's take flight,
Together forging wrongs to right.

Through tangled roots and stormy skies,
We forge ahead, our spirits rise.
Not just words, but truth is found,
On this pathway, we stand unbound.

So let's tread softly, hearts sincere,
Amends await, they draw us near.
With every step, we mend the seams,
On this path of hope, we weave our dreams.

Echoes Beneath the Surface

In the depths, where silence dwells,
Echoes whisper, untold spells.
Ripples form from each lost word,
A symphony that's never heard.

Hidden truths in shadows play,
Lingering softly, day by day.
What we bury, deep inside,
Will surface gently, like the tide.

Listen close to muted tones,
In the stillness, we find our bones.
Faint reminders linger still,
In quiet moments, hearts do fill.

Through the murmur of the night,
Dreams awaken, seeking light.
Each echo a chance to reclaim,
The stories whispered, never the same.

So delve within, embrace what's near,
Let echoes guide, banish fear.
For beneath the stillness, there's a song,
In every heartbeat, we belong.

The Unfolding of Silence

In quiet corners, secrets hide,
The stillness speaks, a gentle guide.
With every pause, the world can breathe,
In silence, we find what we believe.

Fingers trace the void around,
In the hush, the truth is found.
Let thoughts unfurl like petals bright,
In the calm, we seek the light.

Words may falter, but hearts converse,
In silent moments, we disperse.
Every glance a story told,
In the soft embrace, we unfold.

So listen close to what's unsaid,
In the fabric of silence, love is thread.
As laughter ebbs, and tears subside,
In silence, we cannot hide.

With every breath, let silence bloom,
In its garden, we find room.
For in the quiet, connection grows,
The unfolding of silence shows.

Maps of Understanding

In the stillness of the night,
We trace the lines of thought,
With whispers of the stars,
A path we slowly sought.

Every curve and every bend,
Tells tales of where we've been,
With ink of shared regrets,
And dreams that dared to glean.

We gather moments like leaves,
Each memory a spark,
In gardens of our minds,
Where shadows leave their mark.

Through valleys deep and wide,
We wander hand in hand,
Map the heart's terrain,
And forge a bond so grand.

So let us navigate,
With courage as our guide,
In the maps of understanding,
Where love and hope reside.

Lanterns in the Storm

When the winds begin to howl,
And shadows creep in tight,
We lift our lanterns high,
To pierce the folds of night.

Each flicker tells a story,
Of trials we have braved,
With light that holds the darkness,
And keeps our souls enslaved.

Together we stand strong,
In the eye of the fierce gale,
With hearts that beat as one,
Through every daunting trail.

While thunder rumbles low,
And raindrops dance like fire,
Our lanterns softly glow,
As hope climbs ever higher.

So let the tempest roar,
With courage as our song,
For lanterns in the storm,
Will guide us ever long.

Crafting the Sails of Redemption

Beneath the sky of blue,
We gather threads of dawn,
With hands that weave the past,
And dreams that linger on.

Each stitch a whispered promise,
To guide us through the sea,
As we craft the sails of hope,
To set our spirits free.

With every gust of wind,
We rise, we learn, we grow,
The tides that pulled us under,
Now help us onward flow.

Through storms of bitter memories,
We navigate with care,
For sails crafted in forgiveness,
Can lift us from despair.

So let the voyage start,
With sails of pure intent,
For in crafting our redemption,
We find where love is sent.

Through the Cracks of Apology

In the space between our words,
Lie fractures yet to mend,
With echoes of our sorrow,
A bridge we must unbend.

As light seeps through the cracks,
Of all the hurt we cast,
We gather moments lost,
And learn to love at last.

The whispers of our hearts,
Speak softly, though we're strained,
As understanding blossoms,
From every tear we've drained.

With each apology spoken,
We pave a brand new way,
Through cracks of hurt and anger,
Together we will stay.

So let us rebuild trust,
With love as our decree,
For through the cracks of apology,
We find what sets us free.

Reframing the Ineffable

In shadows of thought, we linger still,
Words dance on lips yet fall from will.
Through silence we seek what cannot be shown,
A truth so close, yet wholly unknown.

Veils of perception we gently lift,
Unravel the night, let dawn be the gift.
Each whisper of light, a flicker we trace,
Reflections of all in this timeless space.

In moments we pause, the world fades away,
Infinite echoes in night's soft array.
With hearts wide open, we search and we find,
The language of feelings, unbound and unlined.

Through art and through dream, we venture anew,
To catch the glimmers of things we once knew.
In the stillness we grasp the essence of lore,
Reframed in the heart, forever we explore.

The Ripple of Recognition

In still waters, a stone is cast,
Ripples expand, shifting so vast.
Awakening moments, bright sparks in time,
Echoing laughter, a soft, sweet chime.

With glances exchanged, the world feels anew,
A tapestry woven with threads of the true.
Connections like roots, intertwine and align,
In the depths of our souls, a warmth we define.

Each story unfolds, a shared refrain,
In the rhythm of life, we dance through the rain.
With hearts unguarded, we dare to believe,
In the power of love, we endlessly weave.

The ripple of joy spreads wide with each day,
A circle expanding, come what may.
Through every heartbeat, a truth we embrace,
Together we flourish, together we trace.

A Tapestry of Good Intentions

Threads of compassion, woven just so,
In the fabric of hope, we let our hearts glow.
Each stitch a promise, each knot a pledge,
In kindness we find solace at the edge.

Colors of thought, vibrant and bright,
In the loom of our lives, we create pure light.
The patterns we weave hold stories untold,
In the warmth of connection, love's bounty unfolds.

Winds of change whisper softly through seams,
In the quiet of night, we nurture our dreams.
Together we labor, hand in hand, side by side,
In a tapestry rich where good spirits abide.

Let us gather threads from the past and today,
In the tapestry woven, we'll find our own way.
Each heart is a loom where intentions can grow,
Through the love we give, our true colors show.

Revisiting the Space Between

In the hushed stillness, a pause occurs,
A breath held in time, the universe stirs.
Between each heartbeat, a world we ignite,
Where silence speaks volumes, and shadows take flight.

We dance on the line, the rhythm so fine,
In the margins of life, our spirits entwine.
The moments suspended, like dew on the grass,
Reflecting the beauty where time dares to pass.

In glances exchanged, the resonance grows,
A tapestry woven from how nature flows.
Through the stillness we wander, embracing the chill,
In the space between spaces, our hearts find their fill.

Let us cherish the gaps, the whispers of fate,
In the pause of the world, we learn to wait.
For in the brief quiet, we come to see clear,
The magic resides in the moments we hear.

Shards of Notion

In the quiet of the night,
We gather pieces of thought,
Scattered hopes like starlight,
In dreams, the battles fought.

Fractured views we hold tight,
Reflecting our hidden fears,
Imperfect, yet so bright,
Glimmering through our tears.

Words like glass, sharp and clear,
Cut through silence and despair,
We unite, we cheer,
In the stories that we share.

Together we make a whole,
Building bridges over streams,
With every shard, a role,
In the fabric of our dreams.

So let us forge ahead,
Embrace the pieces we find,
In the tapestry of dread,
Hope and light intertwined.

Tracing Lines of Empathy

In every heart, a story lies,
Every tear, a path to tread,
With open arms, we'll realize,
The ties that weave us instead.

Drawn together by our fate,
Lines of kindness bind us tight,
In the silence, we relate,
With compassion, shine our light.

Footprints on the sands of time,
In the struggles, we connect,
Through the rhythm, we will climb,
Finding ways to resurrect.

With every shared embrace,
We find strength in our design,
In the warmth of a safe space,
Compassion becomes our sign.

So let's trace these lines with care,
Cultivating love and grace,
In the harmony we share,
Together, we can face.

Heartfelt Engagement

With open hearts, we gather near,
Listening to the whispers low,
In the warmth, we feel no fear,
Unified in our flow.

Every voice, a melody,
Telling tales of pain and joy,
In our presence, we can see,
Dreams unbroken, never coy.

Together, we face the storm,
Casting doubt into the sea,
In our passion, we transform,
Building bridges, setting free.

Through the laughter and the tears,
We engage in every way,
Wiping clean each other's fears,
In the light of a brand new day.

So let's stand hand in hand,
With open eyes, embrace,
In this heartfelt, warm band,
Creating a loving space.

Breathe Life into Brokenness

In the fragments, life will spark,
Every crack a chance to mend,
With each breath, we leave a mark,
Hope to brokenness we send.

Through the shadows, light will creep,
Softly touching what was whole,
In the silence, dreams will leap,
Breathing warmth into the soul.

With gentle hands, we'll weave anew,
Threads of kindness, rich and bright,
In the broken, clear and true,
Life emerges from the night.

Hold the pieces, do not fear,
Each one tells a tale so grand,
In the chaos, love draws near,
Together we will take a stand.

So let us breathe, begin the dance,
In the moments that we find,
Breathing life into each chance,
Healing hearts and gentle minds.

Threads of Compassion

In shadows deep where sorrows dwell,
A tender heart begins to swell.
With woven strands of kindness near,
Hope finds a path, it draws us clear.

A gentle word, a soft embrace,
Threads of warmth in every space.
In laughter's echo, pain takes flight,
Compassion's glow ignites the night.

Though storms may rage and hearts may break,
Compassion whispers, 'For love's sake.'
Together, forged from tears and trust,
We rise again, we're strong and just.

With every thread, a story spun,
In our embrace, we are as one.
United through the darkest days,
We paint the world in brighter ways.

Through threads of compassion, we ignite,
A tapestry that holds us tight.
In every stitch, a love so true,
Together we are, me and you.

Repainting the Canvas of Us

With every brush, our colors blend,
A canvas fresh where lines extend.
In strokes of love, we redefine,
The portrait of our hearts aligned.

Once faded hues may come alive,
With every heartbeat, we revive.
A splash of joy, a dash of pain,
In vibrant strokes, our truth remains.

Through trials faced and moments shared,
Each vibrant shade shows that we dared.
To paint our dreams with strokes so bold,
In every hue, our love unfolds.

A masterpiece in progress, see,
A dance of colors, you and me.
Together, we craft our fate anew,
Repainting life in shades so true.

In every line, our story's thread,
With colors bright, no fears to dread.
We'll paint the future, hand in hand,
Rewriting all, our love will stand.

Seeds of Reconciliation

In fields once barren, hope takes root,
With every seed, a gentle shoot.
Tender hearts begin to mend,
Reconciliation, a faithful friend.

With waters pure, we nurture growth,
A bond transformed, we pledge our oath.
From broken soil, we rise again,
In healing grace, we find our Zen.

The past may haunt, but love will bloom,
In gardens bright where light consumes.
Together, tending to the scar,
We grow in strength, we reach the star.

Through whispered winds and gentle rains,
The seeds of peace will break our chains.
From ashes cold, a fire glows,
The roots of love, its power shows.

In every heart, a promise lies,
With open arms, we hear the cries.
Together as one, we'll find the way,
In seeds of love, we choose to stay.

Healing Touch of Honesty

A gentle hand, a truth laid bare,
In honesty, we show we care.
No masks to wear, no shadows cast,
In open hearts, we find our path.

With every word, a bridge we build,
Revealing wounds, our souls are thrilled.
The courage found in being clear,
In honesty, we draw so near.

It takes a strength to face the light,
To speak our truths, to share our fright.
But in that space, we find release,
A healing touch brings us sweet peace.

As petals fall, so does our fear,
In honesty, we hold what's dear.
The bonds we forge, through trust's embrace,
In healing light, we find our place.

With open hearts, we mend the seams,
Through honesty, we weave our dreams.
A tapestry of truth and grace,
In healing touch, we find our space.

The Feathers of Forgiveness

In soft whispers, wounds begin to heal,
Feathers floating, light and surreal.
Hands once clenched, now open wide,
In the embrace of love, we confide.

Burdens lifted, hearts set free,
Unity grows like a mighty tree.
With every tear, a story finds grace,
In shadows of pain, we find our place.

Bridges built on trust so rare,
The weight of grudges, too much to bear.
As sunlight breaks through the gloom,
A garden blooms from seeds of room.

Letting go, a sacred art,
With every beat, mending a heart.
In kindness' embrace, we find our wings,
In the chorus of freedom, forgiveness sings.

A Tribute to Vulnerability

In the silence, true strength is shown,
With every crack, our spirit has grown.
A tender heart bears the weight of truth,
In the laughter of joy and the cries of youth.

Walls come down, let the light seep in,
In the depths of struggle, we learn to begin.
To bare our souls, a daring leap,
In the arms of trust, we learn, we weep.

Each scar tells a story, a badge we wear,
In the tapestry of life, woven with care.
Our fears dissolve in the face of grace,
In vulnerability's arms, we find our place.

Through fragile whispers, we dance and sway,
In the warmth of acceptance, we choose to stay.
Every tear, a river of pain,
In the beauty of openness, there's much to gain.

A Loving Reckoning

In the quiet moments, truth appears,
Through shadows of doubt, we confront our fears.
With gentle eyes, we seek to understand,
In the landscape of love, we make our stand.

Conversations soft, like the evening breeze,
Reckon with hearts that yearn to please.
As memories flash, we choose to forgive,
In the chalice of love, we learn to live.

Stripped of pretense, we embrace the raw,
In vulnerability, we find the law.
For love's a journey, not a race,
In the arms of reckoning, we find our place.

With every word, a bridge we build,
In the sacred space, our souls are filled.
With honesty tender, we find our voice,
In the rhythm of love, we make our choice.

Epistles of Compassion

In the diaries of life, compassion flows,
With ink of kindness, the heart knows.
A letter penned in the depths of care,
In each stroke, the journey we share.

Words like petals, soft and light,
In the darkest hours, they shine bright.
Echoing stories, echoes of truth,
In the warmth of love, we nurture our youth.

With open arms, we gather near,
In the whispers of love, we conquer fear.
A tapestry woven with threads of hope,
In each epistle, we learn to cope.

For compassion blooms where hearts unite,
In the garden of empathy, we ignite.
Each note a promise, a pledge we take,
In the symphony of life, love's song we make.

Ink Blots on a Pained Page

Ink blots scatter like dreams,
Shadows of whispers, muted seams.
A canvas torn with stories told,
Echoes of truths, both brave and bold.

Each drop a mark of hurt and grace,
A testament to a fractured space.
In every smear, a silent plea,
To find a way to set us free.

Pages worn with silent tears,
Ink stains born from hidden fears.
They tell of battles fought alone,
Of hearts that ache, yet still have grown.

A scribbled line, a fractured thought,
Lessons learned and battles fought.
Within the mess, a beauty lies,
A path to heal, a place to rise.

So let the ink flow, let it bleed,
For in these marks, we plant a seed.
In every blot, a chance to mend,
A pained page that learns to bend.

Embracing Vulnerability

In the quiet, hearts unfold,
Hidden truths, bravely told.
Walls come down, fears in sight,
Finding strength in honest light.

A gentle breath, a steady hand,
In the raw, we make our stand.
Trembling voices, soft and clear,
Together we conquer each fear.

With open arms, we face the storm,
In imperfection, we find form.
Layers shed, revealing skin,
In vulnerability, we begin.

Trust is built with each brave step,
In shared moments, secrets kept.
Like tender leaves in springtime air,
In the open, love is laid bare.

So let the world see who we are,
Shining bright like a guiding star.
In every crack, in every flaw,
Together we rise, love as our law.

The Bridge of Understanding

A bridge of words, a quiet space,
Where differences meet with grace.
In shared stories, we find a way,
To break the walls that lead astray.

Listen close, hear the heart's song,
In every note, we all belong.
Bridges built on trust and care,
A journey rich, a love laid bare.

With open minds, we walk the line,
Forging paths that intertwine.
Each step taken, hand in hand,
In understanding, we make our stand.

Empathy's light guides us through,
In every challenge, a chance to renew.
Together we face the unknown tide,
On the bridge, with hearts as our guide.

So let us cherish what we've found,
In the space where souls are unbound.
For understanding makes us whole,
A bridge connecting every soul.

The Language of Apology

Words woven soft, a humble plea,
In whispered tones, we set hearts free.
An olive branch extended wide,
In the language of sorrow, we confide.

Each syllable carries weight and grace,
Restoring trust in a fragile space.
A step towards healing, a gentle mend,
In every apology, a chance to amend.

With open hearts, we take the time,
To find the rhythm, to make it rhyme.
In sincere tones, we bridge the gap,
Finding peace in the tender map.

Forgiveness dances on the breeze,
In shared moments, we find ease.
Like raindrops falling, soft and clear,
The language of apology draws near.

So let us speak with honest hearts,
In each confession, love imparts.
For in this grace, we learn to be,
The language of love, setting us free.

A Chorus of Accords

In the twilight's gentle embrace,
Voices rise without a trace.
Melodies weave through the air,
Filling hearts with dreams to share.

Harmonies dance like light on streams,
Echoing our truest dreams.
Each note a promise, pure and bright,
Guiding us through the night.

In the chorus, we find our way,
Together we stand, come what may.
A symphony of souls in flight,
Creating a world painted in light.

So let the music swell and rise,
Underneath the expansive skies.
In every chord, a heartbeat sings,
A timeless bond that love brings.

United, we reach for the stars,
Beneath the moon, no more scars.
In each measure, peace we find,
A chorus of hearts, beautifully aligned.

Embracing Our Imperfections

In flawed reflections, beauty lies,
A patchwork quilt of tender sighs.
With every crack, our stories flow,
Embracing shadows, letting go.

Our finest lines are those we bear,
Worn like badges, rich and rare.
In our quirks, we find our grace,
A splendid dance, a warm embrace.

Imperfect hearts still beat so strong,
In honesty, we all belong.
With every scar that tells a tale,
We stand together, we won't fail.

In the tapestry of who we are,
Each thread a lesson, a guiding star.
With open arms, we gather near,
Finding strength in what we fear.

So let's celebrate our unique art,
The quirks that make us play our part.
For in this world, both vast and small,
Our imperfections unite us all.

The Reverberation of a Sincere Voice

Whispers echo through the night,
Carried softly, pure delight.
A heartfelt word can change the air,
In every truth, we become aware.

The power of love in gentle tones,
Uniting spirits, breaking bones.
An honest heart can shatter walls,
In the silence, that soft call.

Sincerity wraps like a warm embrace,
Tracing paths in time and space.
With every note, connection grows,
Planting seeds that nature sows.

As voices blend, the world awakes,
In a harmony that never shakes.
Through shared stories, we find our role,
The reverberation of a unified soul.

In laughter's lift and sorrow's strain,
Through every joy, through every pain.
Let's speak our truths, let them ignite,
A symphony to guide through night.

Beneath the Layers of Grief

In shadows deep, our hearts reside,
Beneath the layers, we often hide.
A tender ache, a silent scream,
In every tear, a shattered dream.

Yet in the stillness, strength appears,
To face the storm, to dry the tears.
With each inhale, we find our ground,
In the quiet, hope is found.

Memories linger, dancing slow,
In moments shared, love's afterglow.
Through whispers soft and echoes loud,
We honor sorrow, wear it proud.

And as the seasons shift and turn,
With every loss, a lesson learned.
In grief's embrace, we grow anew,
Finding peace in what we pursue.

So let us walk through vale and pain,
With open hearts, we'll dance in rain.
For underneath the weight we bear,
Beneath our grief lies love to share.

Mosaics of Remorse

Shattered dreams on the floor,
Each piece tells a tale.
Faded colors of regret,
Echoes of a lost trail.

Heart heavy with the weight,
Memories wrapped in pain.
Reflections in the glass,
Tell stories like the rain.

Woven in the silence,
Guilt lingers in the air.
A canvas of remorse,
Where hope finds it hard to dare.

Fragments of what could be,
Scattered all around.
In the stillness, they breathe,
The sorrow knows no sound.

Yet amidst the shadows,
A glimmer starts to rise.
From pieces of the past,
A new future lies.

Sculpting New Beginnings

In the warmth of the dawn,
Clay waits for gentle hands.
Ideas swirl like the breeze,
Ready to meet new plans.

Every touch brings a spark,
Shaping dreams into form.
Chiseling away the doubt,
Creating through the storm.

Pushing boundaries aside,
With courage, we define.
Molding fears into strength,
In a world that's so fine.

Layers build with each try,
Foundations firm and true.
Sculpting with intention,
Crafting what is new.

As the day fades to night,
The work reveals its soul.
In every curve, a story,
In each piece, we are whole.

Heartbeat of an Honest Soul

In whispers of the night,
Truth dances in the dark.
A pulse that speaks of love,
Leaving its gentle mark.

With every shared heartbeat,
Promises flutter near.
A bond forged in the light,
Reflects what we hold dear.

Every laugh, every sigh,
Restores the faith we seek.
In moments raw and real,
The silent words we speak.

In the chaos of the day,
Hearts find a shared song.
A symphony of souls,
Where we truly belong.

Hands reach out in kindness,
In softness, we unite.
Each heartbeat, a reminder,
That honesty feels right.

Threads of Empathy

Woven in the fabric,
Stitches hold us tight.
In colors of compassion,
We find our shared light.

Each story tells a tale,
Of struggles borne with grace.
Threads of understanding,
Stitch together our space.

Listening with our hearts,
Voices intertwine.
A tapestry of hope,
In each delicate line.

Through the storms of life,
We gather what we can.
With every thread we share,
We create a new plan.

In the warmth of togetherness,
We mend what is torn.
Threads of empathy unite,
In a world reborn.

Letters Never Sent

In a drawer they lie, untouched,
Words of love and pain, unsaid,
Ink fading with each passing day,
Whispers of a heart misled.

Promises wrapped in silence,
Dreams drifting in the night,
Pages filled with what could be,
Yet never brought to light.

Time moves on, as seasons change,
Memories fade like distant stars,
What once felt so urgent,
Now seems like forgotten scars.

Regrets linger in the stillness,
Unwritten letters haunt my pen,
Ghosts of thoughts lost in shadows,
Endless echoes without end.

But still, I speak in quiet tones,
To the pages I never sent,
With each line, I find a piece,
Of my soul, my heart's lament.

A Dialogue of Discontent

Two voices clash in dim-lit rooms,
Words sharp as blades, full of spite,
What once was warmth is now a chill,
A dance of shadows, day and night.

Every sentence drips with caution,
Fences built on fears and doubt,
Clarity lost in the murmur,
Understanding, a fading shout.

Fractured dreams in whispered tones,
Each pause heavy, thick with pain,
What we loved begins to wither,
Under the weight of disdain.

Yet beneath the sighs and tension,
A flicker of hope remains,
For buried deep, a longing stirs,
To break these sorrowed chains.

Can we find a softer language,
One that bends but won't break?
In the silence, deep connections,
Might just be ours to make.

Eclipsed by Misunderstandings

In shadows cast by unspoken words,
We drift apart, a silent tide,
What once was clear now feels obscure,
In tangled thoughts we try to hide.

Your eyes tell tales I cannot read,
While silence screams between us two,
The moon eclipses every spark,
Of light we wished we always knew.

Missteps linger in the echoes,
Of laughter lost in tangled fate,
Each glance a question, never voiced,
Lost in mistakes we cannot rate.

Days stretch thin like fragile threads,
Connecting hearts but fraying fast,
Time weaves a tapestry of haste,
Of moments we wished would last.

Yet somewhere still, a glimmer glows,
A chance for us to understand,
If we can bridge this silent gap,
We might just find a common strand.

Beneath the Ashes of Hurt

In the aftermath of what was lost,
Embers flicker in the quiet night,
Once vibrant flames now turn to dust,
Hidden deep, beneath the fight.

Grief settles like a heavy veil,
Obscuring joy, sharpening pain,
Yet beneath the ashes, hope still breathes,
A flickering urge to start again.

Each scar tells stories of the past,
Of battles fought and bridges burned,
Yet each wound has shaped a journey,
From every lesson, we have learned.

As the winds shift and time moves on,
We find strength in what remains,
From ashes rise the blooms of life,
In fragile beauty, love regains.

So let us sift through dust and dreams,
Reclaim what once was pure and bright,
For beneath the ashes lies the truth,
A new beginning in the night.

Whispers of Regret

In the quiet hours of night,
Memories cling like shadows,
Regrets weave a tangled thread,
Whispers echo through the soul.

Each choice lingers in the air,
A ghost that softly mourns,
Paths untaken whisper low,
Voices lost in heavy clouds.

Promises that slipped away,
Fate's cruel hand weaves despair,
Time dances on a brittle stage,
With every step, a sigh escapes.

Haunted by what could have been,
Silent screams within the heart,
Every dawn brings fresh remorse,
Yet hope flickers in the dark.

In every tear a story lies,
Lessons learned in echoes deep,
Embrace the whispers, let them guide,
For in the pain, we truly weep.

Canvas of Sorrow

Brush strokes of a heavy heart,
Paint the canvas with my tears,
Colors blend in shades of gray,
Each hue tells a tale of fears.

Every line a story etched,
Of love lost and paths unclear,
The weight of sorrow on my chest,
Whispers linger, ever near.

A palette filled with aching dreams,
Fragments scattered in the mist,
Each drop of paint a memory,
Captured moments we can't resist.

The canvas weeps in silent strokes,
Framed by shadows of the past,
Yet from the sorrow, beauty grows,
In every line, a love that's cast.

In the gallery of my mind,
Each painting sings its lonely tune,
A canvas laden with my soul,
Forever lost beneath the moon.

Inked in Remorse

Words spill like ink upon the page,
Telling tales of deep regret,
Each sentence a heavy weight,
Stories etched that I can't forget.

Lines of sorrow intertwine,
Reflecting all the paths I've strayed,
In every word, a piece of me,
Seeking solace, yet dismayed.

The quill, it trembles in my grasp,
As memories rush like a tide,
Flowing ink fills every empty space,
A testament to love denied.

With every stroke, the past unfolds,
Each paragraph a silent plea,
Inked in remorse, I lay it bare,
Hoping for a chance to be free.

In this script, I find my truth,
A journey through the pain I face,
Inked in remorse, yet still I write,
For in the sadness, I find grace.

Echoes of a Sorry Heart

In the chambers of my heart,
Echoes whisper soft and low,
Each beat a reminder sweet,
Of loves that faded, lost in woe.

Sorry sighs drift on the breeze,
Carried far away from me,
Yet still they linger, bittersweet,
A haunting song of memory.

With every echo, lessons learned,
In the silence, truths resound,
Forgive the past and set it free,
But sorrow still hangs all around.

A heart once full now bears the scars,
Each echo tells of battles fought,
In the twilight, I find my peace,
As shadows dance with dreams I sought.

In echoes of a sorry heart,
Resilience blooms, a fragile start,
For in the depths of darkest night,
Hope flickers, healing every part.

The Long Road to Redemption

Through shadows deep and valleys wide,
I walk alone with weary stride.
Each step a whisper of my past,
A journey long, the die is cast.

With every turn, the light grows faint,
Yet hope ignites where dreams can paint.
The weight of sins, a heavy load,
But forward still, I'll trace my road.

The fallen leaves, they mark the way,
A testament to yesterday.
Yet in the dusk of fading light,
I seek the dawn, a new insight.

From ashes rise, I shed my shame,
In deep despair, I found my flame.
Redemption calls, a voice so clear,
It guides me through the trembles near.

Beneath the stars, I lift my face,
In every tear, I find my grace.
The long road bends, but I shall stand,
With open heart, I take my hand.

A Serenade for the Sorrowful

In twilight's hush, the sorrow sings,
A melody the heart still brings.
Each note a tear, each chord a sigh,
A symphony for those who cry.

The shadows dance on walls of gold,
With whispers soft, the stories told.
In every heart, a silent plea,
For solace found in harmony.

The rain begins to gently fall,
A rhythm sweet that soothes us all.
The world in grey, a canvas stark,
Yet hope ignites, a radiant spark.

Through sleepless nights, the song persists,
A haunting tune that can't be missed.
With every breath, we fade, we cling,
To fragile dreams the night can bring.

Oh, sorrow sweet, you teach us well,
To find the strength in every swell.
A serenade for hearts in pain,
A cage of hurt, now breaks the chain.

Palettes of Pain and Healing

A canvas spread, with colors bright,
Mixing hues of shadow, light.
Each stroke a tale of love and loss,
A tapestry that bears the cross.

From crimson reds of fevered fights,
To soft blues of endless nights,
A palette rich with depths unseen,
Where pain and healing intervene.

In golden swirls, the laughter glows,
Among the grays, the sorrow flows.
The brush, it dances on the page,
A story woven, heart's engage.

Each layer thick, with memories bare,
An artist's heart, laid out with care.
Yet through the dark, the colors burst,
In every hue, the moment cursed.

For healing comes in shades of time,
A quiet rhythm, a silent rhyme.
With every stroke, the past release,
And from the chaos, find the peace.

Gentle Hands of Reconciliation

With gentle hands, we weave the thread,
Of broken dreams and words unsaid.
The fabric worn, yet seams align,
In tender touch, we seek to bind.

Each hand a bridge, each heart a guide,
Through tangled paths where we reside.
In every gesture, peace can grow,
As love ignites the healing glow.

The past may bruise, but hope will mend,
With every touch, we find a friend.
The echo of our voices soft,
In whispered truths, we lift aloft.

From shattered trust to bonds restored,
With open hearts, we can afford.
The grace to see beyond the pain,
And where it hurts, we'll try again.

Oh, gentle hands that teach us love,
To rise again, like stars above.
In every clasp, a story told,
Of reconciliation, brave and bold.

When Silence Speaks

In the hush of night, whispers flow,
Words unspoken, hearts in tow.
Each sigh a story, soft and deep,
Where silence lingers, secrets keep.

Echoes of memories, fading light,
Promises linger, shadows ignite.
In quiet moments, truths unfold,
A language of warmth, a tale retold.

Beneath the moon, we stand alone,
Silence wraps us, like a stone.
Unraveled intentions, tangled fate,
Where words are lost, and time can wait.

The heart listens, though the mind forgets,
A symphony of sighs, no regrets.
In stillness, we find what's left unsaid,
When silence speaks, all fears are shed.

Broken Vows and Mended Hearts

Once we danced in dreams of gold,
A promise made, a love to hold.
Yet time unraveled, threads of trust,
In the ashes, dreams turned to dust.

Whispers lingered, echoes of pain,
Promises shattered, like glass in rain.
But from the ruins, hope takes flight,
For mended hearts can still ignite.

Through the storm, through the night,
We find the spark, a flickering light.
In the fragments, beauty remains,
Overcoming sorrow, love regains.

Forgiveness blooms in gentle ways,
Softening edges, dimming the blaze.
Together we rise, hand in hand,
Building bridges on the sand.

Broken vows can lead to grace,
In every tear, we find our place.
Though scars remain, we choose to start,
In the dance of love, we mend our hearts.

Tides of Forgiveness

The ocean whispers in gentle sighs,
Carrying burdens under vast skies.
In waves that crash, and tides that blend,
Forgiveness flows, a timeless friend.

With every surge, we let it go,
Like footprints washed, they fade, they flow.
The heart learns to heal, to renew,
In the embrace of the deep, so true.

Salt in the air, hope on the shore,
Lessons learned, forevermore.
In serenity's grip, we find our fight,
With tides of forgiveness, day and night.

Beneath the stars, we dare to dream,
In the stillness, we hear the stream.
Of love and loss, of pain and peace,
In ebb and flow, we find release.

So let the waves carry away,
The burdens we've borne, come what may.
In the water's depth, we rediscover,
The beauty of life, like no other.

A Lament in Starlight

Under the vast and silent sky,
We lay beneath the stars that sigh.
Each one a tear, a memory lost,
In the quiet night, we bear the cost.

The universe listens, aches of the heart,
In shadows and light, we play our part.
Each twinkle a story, a dream once bright,
Echoing sorrows, a lament in starlight.

With every comet that streaks so fast,
We capture moments; hold them, last.
In whispered wishes, we weave our fate,
As the galaxy cradles what we create.

Hope flickers gently, like a distant flame,
In the vastness we feel, yet the same.
For starlit nights, though filled with pain,
Bring solace and peace, again and again.

So let the cosmos take our strife,
In the stillness of night, we seek new life.
In each lament, a lesson to find,
Under the stars, we're forever intertwined.

Notes from the Heart's Archive

In pages worn with time's embrace,
Whispers echo of a tender place.
Memories penned in a lover's hand,
Dreams that drift like grains of sand.

Each line unfolds a story dear,
A melody only hearts can hear.
Trust held tight in silken thread,
Beliefs in love, softly spread.

Yet shadows loom where light retreats,
Faded hopes in quiet beats.
A flicker of joy, a flicker of pain,
Ink stains linger like autumn rain.

But still I write, with heart in tow,
Scripting love that's rich and slow.
In every verse a piece of me,
Notes from the heart, wild and free.

The Weight of Unsaid Words

Between the lines, the silence grows,
A burden wrapped in tender prose.
What could be said, forever stays,
In shadowed corners, lost in haze.

A single glance, a fleeting sigh,
In moments lost, we wonder why.
Words unspoken, heavy as stone,
Remnants of feelings we can't condone.

A wall of doubt, a veil so thin,
Each unvoiced thought, a silent sin.
The words we save, the truth we bend,
A cycle of longing with no end.

Yet still we hope in whispered tones,
To free the heart from reason's drones.
In quiet moments, bravery stirs,
And lifts the weight of unsaid words.

A Lament of Lost Trust

In shattered fragments, trust resides,
A silent echo, where love divides.
Promises fray at the edges thin,
A dance of hope, where shame begins.

Each secret kept, a blade in time,
Carving walls in reason's rhyme.
Once forged in fire, now cold and grey,
A bond unraveled, drifting away.

Yet within the pain, there lies a choice,
To mend the rift, to find the voice.
To navigate through the darkest night,
And seek the dawn, to find the light.

For trust can bloom from broken dreams,
A patchwork quilt of daring schemes.
With courage kindled, we may begin,
To weave anew where we once have been.

Unraveling the Threads of Hurt

In tangled webs of sorrow spun,
We search for peace when day is done.
Each thread a tale of pain and grace,
A fabric worn, yet we embrace.

With gentle hands, we pull apart,
To find the fibers that bind the heart.
What once was whole, now frays with time,
An intricate dance of muted rhyme.

We sit in silence, ghosts of the past,
Finding solace in memories cast.
Yet healing comes in whispered sighs,
A soft reminder beneath vast skies.

And as we weave the stories told,
New patterns form, a tapestry bold.
In every tear, a seed of hope,
To guide our hearts, help us to cope.

The Weight of a Silent Tear

In the stillness of night, shadows creep,
Heavy hearts gather, secrets they keep.
A tear slips away, lost in the dark,
Silent whispers echo, leaving their mark.

Memories linger, haunting and near,
Each drop tells a story, laced with fear.
A burden so deep, unseen to the eye,
Hopes crushed beneath the weight of a sigh.

Time slips like sand, through fingers it flows,
Yet this silent tear, only the heart knows.
Awakening dreams that flutter and fade,
In silence they linger, in silence they wade.

Though the world spins on, the pain remains,
A silent tear falls, holding its chains.
Each droplet a promise, unbroken, yet real,
The weight of a tear, the depth of its feel.

In the Shadow of Remorse

In the quiet moments, regrets unfold,
Shadows of choices, dark and bold.
Whispers of actions that cannot be changed,
In the shadow of remorse, all feels estranged.

Each step taken forward, laced with a sigh,
Echoes of laughter that now seem to die.
In the corners of memory, guilt takes its hold,
Painting the past in colors of cold.

The heart knows the truth, yet longs for the light,
To break free from burdens that haunt in the night.
But back in the shadows, the past does reside,
In the stillness of sorrow, remorse cannot hide.

To seek out redemption, a flicker of hope,
Wandering through darkness, learning to cope.
Each lesson a thread, weaving through pain,
In the shadow of remorse, growth can remain.

Canvas Stains of Contrition

On canvas adorned, shades start to blend,
Colors of chaos, where stories extend.
Each stroke a confession, whispers of shame,
Canvas stains of contrition, a painter's claim.

With brushes dipped deep in the ink of regret,
Every mark tells a tale that time won't forget.
In hues of the heart, a struggle is found,
As feelings collide, a symphony sounds.

Swirling in patterns, the sorrow takes shape,
Painting the truth, seeking to escape.
But art holds a mirror, reflecting the core,
A canvas of feelings, yearning for more.

To layer the colors, to build and renew,
Each stroke of contrition brings hope to the hue.
As the painting unfolds, forgiveness can grow,
In the canvas of life, let love be the flow.

A Dance with Redemption

In the twilight's glow, shadows begin to sway,
A dance with redemption, leading the way.
Feet lightly tread on the edge of despair,
With every soft step, a chance to repair.

The music that plays, a tender embrace,
Guiding the lost to a sacred place.
In rhythm and grace, the heart finds its beat,
As souls intertwine, becoming complete.

Walls once so high, now crumble and fall,
In this dance of redemption, we rise from the stalls.
Each twirl breaks the chains that once held us tight,
Embracing the dawn, we step into light.

With hands held together, the past fades away,
As hope fills the air, we learn how to play.
A dance with redemption, in jubilant cheer,
Celebrating the journey, and conquering fear.

Garden of Second Chances

In the garden where hopes renew,
Seeds of dreams begin to sprout.
Beneath the sun, drenched in dew,
Each petal whispers, 'Don't live in doubt.'

A twist of fate, a gentle breeze,
Faded memories start to bloom.
Through tangled vines, we find our peace,
And banish shadows from the room.

Every flower tells a tale,
Of love lost and what remains.
With every breath, we set our sail,
Navigating through joys and pains.

In this sanctuary of embrace,
Hope fills the air with fragrant light.
A healing touch, a warm embrace,
In the garden, wrongs turn right.

So plant your heart and watch it grow,
With tender care, make it thrive.
In the garden, we come to know,
Life's precious gifts keep dreams alive.

Violin Strings and Broken Melodies

In the silence, a note does plead,
A story woven in sadness sweet.
Strings resonate with every need,
Emotions played with trembling heat.

With every bow, a heart laid bare,
Echoes dance in the empty hall.
Broken rhythms of love and care,
Each harmony whispers our fall.

Yet within the fractured sound,
A beauty hides, soft and profound.
In dissonance, we are all found,
Lessons taught, yet unbound.

Bridges built from aching strings,
From sorrow, new symphonies rise.
Love's refrain, as the heart sings,
In pain, we find a sweet disguise.

So play the tune, let it unfold,
Through every crack, a light will shine.
In brokenness, a truth is told,
Violin strings, our paths align.

The Chisel of Compassion

With every chip, the stone reveals,
A form beneath the rugged face.
The chisel of compassion heals,
Crafting beauty, leaving grace.

Hands that shape with tender care,
A sculptor's heart, both strong and kind.
In kindness, we find strength to bear,
Understanding paths intertwined.

Through trials faced, in shadows cast,
A carving softens, grief aligned.
Each fragment speaks of love amassed,
In every piece, new hope we find.

With each stroke, our spirits rise,
In unity, our burdens shared.
The chisel hears our silent cries,
In compassion, we are bared.

So let us mold the world anew,
With hearts as tools, a vibrant trust.
In every shape, a vision true,
The chisel of compassion must.

Heartstrings Entwined in Guilt

In the echoes of a fading night,
Heartstrings pull with haunting cries.
A whisper lost in shadows' flight,
Guilt lingers in unspoken sighs.

The weight of words never expressed,
Tangles tight, like vines that bind.
In silence, our souls feel distressed,
In love's shadow, we are blind.

Through memories, sharp as glass,
Regret weaves a painful thread.
In every moment, time will pass,
Yet guilt resides in all we dread.

Release the bonds, learn to forgive,
In the heart lies a fragile light.
To live is to feel, to truly live,
Beneath the stars, reclaim the night.

So let the heartstrings find their song,
Entwined with love, let go of fear.
In the journey, we all belong,
With every heartbeat, crystal clear.

Steps Towards Truce

In the shadow of the night,
We whisper soft and low,
A path together, step by step,
To heal what was once woe.

Hands entwined, we breathe as one,
Breaking walls that time has built,
With each word, we cross the line,
Dissolving pain, our guilt.

Let our voices rise like dawn,
Through the mist, a song appears,
Hope ignites the darkened space,
Washing away past fears.

As we walk, the past unwinds,
Each moment shared, a thread,
Stitching hearts and mending minds,
With every tear we've shed.

Together, we will forge a path,
Toward the light that breaks the night,
In this truce, we find our strength,
Emerging from our fight.

Distilled Answers from the Heart

In silence deep, we search for truth,
A journey to our core,
Where love and wisdom intertwine,
Awaiting us to explore.

Each question pressed against the soul,
Like whispers on the breeze,
The answers bloom, a gentle glow,
In moments full of ease.

With every beat, the heart confides,
Its stories etched in time,
Where joy and sorrow coexist,
In rhythms, pure and prime.

Let honesty flow like a stream,
Distilling fears away,
In vulnerability, we find,
The light of a new day.

Through open eyes, we see the light,
Reflecting all we seek,
For within each tender gaze,
The answers softly speak.

The Healing of Wounded Souls

In the depths of pain we dwell,
Yet hope begins to rise,
With every tear, a story told,
In the silence, wise.

Through gentle hands, we find our way,
Embracing what we've lost,
Each scar a mark of battles fought,
Measuring the cost.

Together, hearts rebuild anew,
In trust, we softly mend,
Finding strength in shared embrace,
Where broken paths can end.

The light seeps in, a tender balm,
As wounds begin to close,
In the warmth of understanding,
Compassion blooms and grows.

With time, the shadows fade away,
Transformed into the light,
For every soul that's wounded,
Can find its way to flight.

Portraits of Empathy

In every eye, a story waits,
A canvas full of dreams,
With shades of joy and shades of pain,
Life's intricate themes.

As we pause to share the heart,
Compassion paints each scene,
Brushing strokes of understanding,
In spaces, soft and serene.

We hear the echoes of their lives,
In laughter and in tears,
The colors blend, a vibrant hue,
Creating bonds through years.

Let empathy be our guiding star,
Illuminating the night,
As we embrace each portrait drawn,
With love as our light.

Together, we can weave a tale,
Of kindness, strong and bold,
In every heart, a masterpiece,
In portraits to behold.

A Quest for True Remorse

In shadows deep, where silence dwells,
The heart bears weight, a solemn tale.
Each whispered word, a spell that swells,
As lost regrets weave through the veil.

To seek the truths that haunt the night,
With courage bold, I make my plea.
In yearning hearts, there's fragile light,
A chance to mend what's gone from me.

Through twisted paths, the echoes ring,
Their moaning ties, a ghostly chain.
Yet in the dark, the dawn will spring,
As hope awakens from the pain.

I search for peace, a quiet grace,
To softly heal the scars I hold.
In every tear, a sacred space,
Where love, once lost, is re-enrolled.

So onward still, this quest I face,
To find the way, my heart explored.
With every step, a new embrace,
In true remorse, my spirit soared.

Finding Clarity in Confession

In whispered tones, the truth unfolds,
A burden lost, a heart laid bare.
With every word, a weight that holds,
The light of dawn begins to care.

Beneath the mask, the soul is found,
Each secret shared, a gentle breeze.
In shared confessions, bonds are crowned,
As honesty brings hearts to ease.

The shadows dance, but light persists,
Together we, in grace, revive.
No fear can haunt, no pain resist,
In clarity, our spirits thrive.

As rivers flow, our stories blend,
In currents deep, we swim anew.
With every truth, we start to mend,
Confessions shared, our hearts so true.

So here we stand, both raw and free,
Unraveled threads in woven fates.
With every word, there is a key,
In shared release, the love awaits.

The Hearth of Understanding

Within the glow of embered flame,
We gather close, our voices low.
In warmth and light, we stake our claim,
A place where hearts and thoughts can flow.

Each story shared a cherished gift,
A binding force that draws us near.
With every word, old walls can shift,
In understanding, we conquer fear.

Through joyful laughs and softened sighs,
Connections formed, a tapestry.
We find the truth behind the lies,
In every glance, a mystery.

With fragile hands, we shape the night,
Creating bonds that won't decay.
In every tale, both wrong and right,
The hearth of understanding stays.

As shadows dance, we brave the night,
In unity, our spirits soar.
Together bound by love's own light,
At this warm hearth, we are restored.

Frayed Bonds

Once woven tight, now threads unwind,
A tapestry of memories frayed.
In whispered truths, the heart can find,
What once was bright, now fades away.

The laughter shared, now echoes faint,
Each moment passed, a ghostly wail.
Yet in the scars, we learn to paint,
A brand new path beyond the pale.

Through tangled roots that twist and bind,
Emerges strength, we shall not break.
With every tear, the heart will grind,
And from the wreck, new dreams will wake.

In shadows cast, a spark of light,
To guide us through the darkest days.
Though frayed, these bonds are worth the fight,
For love will bloom in tangled ways.

So here we stand, though worn and tried,
In every flaw, a lesson learned.
Together still, our hearts abide,
As new connections softly churned.

Fresh Starts

In gentle dawn, a promise brews,
With every step, a path unfolds.
As night recedes, our spirits choose,
To break the chains, embrace the bold.

With open hearts, we shed the past,
And carry dreams like morning dew.
A chance to grow, to heal, to last,
In every sunrise, we renew.

The scars of old may linger still,
Yet in their wake, new strength will rise.
With every breath, intent and will,
We find the stars within our skies.

With hope as guide and love as light,
We step unbowed into the fray.
For fresh starts shine, both bold and bright,
A canvas stretched for dreams to play.

So here we stand, with open arms,
In every heartbeat, life's embrace.
Through turns and trials, we find our charms,
In fresh beginnings, time and space.

Forging Bonds Beyond Blame

In the fire of discord, we stand side by side,
With the weight of our burdens, our spirits abide.
Through the heat of our trials, we learn to be strong,
Forging bonds unbroken, where we both belong.

In the sparks of our laughter, the shadows retreat,
Finding strength in our voices, our hearts will compete.
Hand in hand with resolve, we rise from the ash,
Forging bonds beyond blame, our love will not crash.

Learning from our scars, we dance in the light,
Together we wander, embracing the fight.
With each step we take, we weave a new thread,
Forging bonds unyielding, our hearts shall be fed.

Through moments of silence, we cherish the pain,
With every regret, a lesson we gain.
In the depth of our sorrow, we find the way through,
Forging bonds that will last, pure, honest, and true.

So let us remember, in each fleeting glance,
That love is the rhythm, our perfect dance.
With a heart full of courage, we'll turn back the tide,
Forging bonds beyond blame, forever side by side.

The Palette of Unraveled Emotions

With brushes of sorrow, we paint our own fate,
In hues of affection, where love does await.
Each stroke tells a story, both vivid and bright,
The palette of feelings, a canvas of light.

In shades of confusion, we learn to define,
The depth of our yearnings, our spirits entwined.
A blend of raw moments, let colors collide,
The palette of unspoken, where secrets reside.

With whispers of passion, we capture the night,
As colors blend softly, our hearts take their flight.
In the warmth of the sunset, emotions ablaze,
The palette of loving, in myriad ways.

Through storms of despair, we find strength in the art,
Each canvas a window, a glimpse of the heart.
Together we create, with each brush and each tear,
The palette of memories, both precious and dear.

So let us embrace, all the colors we share,
In the tapestry of life, we find beauty rare.
With every emotion, our spirits will grow,
The palette of unpainted, our love it will show.

Whispers of Regret

In the still of the night, silent thoughts invade,
Whispers of regret in the shadows are laid.
With echoes of choices we wish to erase,
In the corners of memory, they softly embrace.

A glance in the mirror reveals all the pain,
The weight of each moment, like drops of the rain.
Yet within these regrets, a lesson is found,
A chance to reflect, where hope can rebound.

Through words left unspoken, and ties that we broke,
Whispers of regret linger, lost in the smoke.
But as dawn brings its light, our hearts start to mend,
Finding solace in knowing this isn't the end.

So let us not wallow in shadows of shame,
For the whispers of regret can ignite a new flame.
With courage to change, and a heart open wide,
We rise from the ashes, with love as our guide.

In the depths of our sorrow, we learn to forgive,
With whispers of hope, our spirits will live.
Embracing each moment, let go of the fret,
In the silence of night, we find peace in regret.

Echoes of Forgiveness

In the chambers of time, where the heart learns to heal,
Echoes of forgiveness, the truth we conceal.
With each soft embrace, we release all the pain,
And find in forgiveness, our spirits regain.

In the silence of sorrow, two souls intertwine,
With whispers of love that gracefully shine.
A journey we share through the valleys of doubt,
Echoes of forgiveness, from within, they shout.

Through shadows of anger, we wander and seek,
In the power of kindness, our hearts become meek.
With every soft word, and each gesture sincere,
Echoes of forgiveness, bringing warmth, drawing near.

So let go of the burdens, release what has bound,
With echoes of compassion, new paths we have found.
Through the tides of the past, we embrace the unknown,
Echoes of forgiveness, together we've grown.

As dawn breaks anew, let our hearts intertwine,
With the promise of healing, our spirits align.
In the dance of redemption, let our voices unite,
Echoes of forgiveness, guiding us into light.

A Canvas of Sorrow

Colors bleed, like tears that fall,
Each stroke whispers, a silent call.
Shadows dance upon the wall,
A heart's lament, the canvas small.

Distant echoes haunt the night,
Memories flicker, lost in flight.
Life's palette, dark and bright,
A tapestry of wrong and right.

Fragments of dreams float away,
Captured moments, turn to gray.
Caught between the night and day,
Hope and despair, in disarray.

Brushes tremble, laden with doubt,
Concealed feelings scream and shout.
Creation born from fear, no route,
Each layer hides what life's about.

Yet in sorrow's deep embrace,
Lies the spark to find our place.
A canvas holds, with gentle grace,
The beauty found in our heartfelt trace.

Healing Through the Void

In the silence, where echoes fade,
A formless dance, where dreams invade.
Whispers linger in the shade,
Hope arises, not afraid.

Floating in a sea of stars,
Wounds begin to mend their scars.
Guided by the light from afar,
Finding peace in who we are.

Each breath taken, a step anew,
Through empty spaces, strength we grew.
In darkness, visions start to brew,
The universe, a sacred view.

Like fragile wings that start to soar,
Love emerges, opens the door.
Filling voids we can't ignore,
A journey real, to heal and explore.

Together we rise from the ground,
In shared silence, healing found.
Through the void, we're tightly bound,
A melody of hope resounds.

Mending Broken Bonds

Frayed edges in a woven thread,
Words unspoken, softly tread.
Once united, now misled,
Hope remains where love is spread.

Hands reach out, across the space,
Bridges built, in time and grace.
Through the storms, we find our place,
Healing hearts in warm embrace.

Each moment shared, a gentle sway,
In the garden, where we play.
From the ashes, bright as day,
Growing love to light the way.

With each laughter, shadows fade,
Gentle whispers, promises made.
In this dance, the heart displayed,
Together strong, we'll never trade.

Through the trials, bonds refine,
In the breaks, new paths align.
Mending hearts, and souls entwine,
A tapestry of love divine.

Words Woven in Grace

With gentle hands, we spin the word,
In soft whispers, truth is heard.
Stories linger, chords stirred,
Each line a note, sweetly interred.

In the silence, echoes play,
Crafting wisdom in our stay.
Through the night, and dawning day,
Words of love will lead the way.

From heart to heart, a thread entwined,
In the warmth, our souls aligned.
Carving pathways, intertwined,
Finding solace, in words defined.

Each verse a tapestry of light,
Guiding lost souls through the night.
In every challenge, find the fight,
Words woven, a shining sight.

So let us share the tales we know,
In quiet moments, let them flow.
For in our hearts, connections grow,
Words woven in grace, ever aglow.